MW01166830

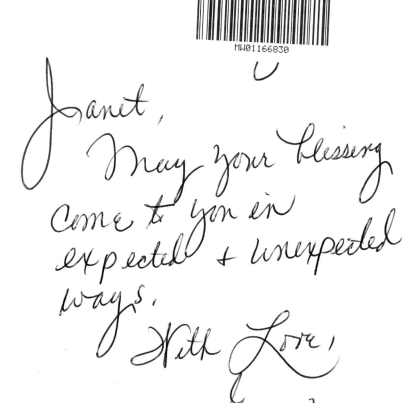

Janet,

May your blessing
come to you in
expected + unexpected
ways.

With Love,

Gwen

POCKET PRAYERS

Inspiration for Daily Living

G WENDOLYN   R OBERTS

BALBOA.
PRESS

A DIVISION OF HAY HOUSE

Copyright © 2015 Gwendolyn Roberts.

All rights reserved. No part of this book may be used or reproduced by
any means, graphic, electronic, or mechanical, including photocopying,
recording, taping or by any information storage retrieval system
without the written permission of the publisher except in the case
of brief quotations embodied in critical articles and reviews.

Balboa Press books may be ordered through booksellers or by contacting:

Balboa Press
A Division of Hay House
1663 Liberty Drive
Bloomington, IN 47403
www.balboapress.com
1 (877) 407-4847

Because of the dynamic nature of the Internet, any web addresses or
links contained in this book may have changed since publication and
may no longer be valid. The views expressed in this work are solely those
of the author and do not necessarily reflect the views of the publisher,
and the publisher hereby disclaims any responsibility for them.

The author of this book does not dispense medical advice or prescribe the use
of any technique as a form of treatment for physical, emotional, or medical
problems without the advice of a physician, either directly or indirectly. The
intent of the author is only to offer information of a general nature to help
you in your quest for emotional and spiritual well-being. In the event you use
any of the information in this book for yourself, which is your constitutional
right, the author and the publisher assume no responsibility for your actions.

Any people depicted in stock imagery provided by Thinkstock are
models, and such images are being used for illustrative purposes only.
Certain stock imagery © Thinkstock.

Print information available on the last page.

ISBN: 978-1-5043-3838-7 (sc)
ISBN: 978-1-5043-3840-0 (hc)
ISBN: 978-1-5043-3839-4 (e)

Library of Congress Control Number: 2015912772

Balboa Press rev. date: 8/18/2015

DEDICATION

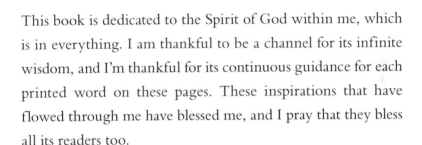

This book is dedicated to the Spirit of God within me, which is in everything. I am thankful to be a channel for its infinite wisdom, and I'm thankful for its continuous guidance for each printed word on these pages. These inspirations that have flowed through me have blessed me, and I pray that they bless all its readers too.

I thank my parents, Lillian and JC, for providing me with a happy and safe childhood. Thank you for letting me come to this planet as your child. Thank you for protecting me and keeping me safe even when as a teenager I wanted to make other choices. Thank you for encouragement and guiding me into adulthood. I hope you are proud.

I extend my greatest appreciation to my wonderful God-sent husband, Bruce, for his love, support, and encouragement as I spent time writing this book. During this time he ate many leftover meals and performed many chores around the house. Thank you, Honey, for being in my life.

I thank my son, Brandon, who most of this time was in college, but was always supportive and helpful by giving me the advice that I gave him: "Stick with it, Mom." Thanks, Brandon, for sharing your computer skills with me when I did not have any idea of how to fix the problem. I am so very proud of you, and I love you dearly.

I also thank my wonderful and insightful brother Malcolm for the long spiritual talks about life that are very inspirational to me.

I include in my dedication of this book my older brother James, who has made his transition. I thank you, James, for further developing my compassion for others with challenging lives.

I thank my many family members and friends that were channels of God, telling me to write a book of the ideas in which I believe and use in my life. I especially thank my sister, Sandra, and friends Vivian and Deanie for lovingly tolerating me telling them to watch their words, "Don't say that; you do not want to manifest that in your life."

It is with this dedication that I desire all of you, my loving friends and family, to know that I love and appreciate each of you dearly. I thank God for placing me with you. I know it is all part of the divine design of my life. Because of you, I am who I am today.

CONTENTS

INTRODUCTION

T his book is written for all who have chosen to develop and bring into fullness their spiritual growth, development, and awareness.

It is my desire that through these daily inspirations you enhance and embrace your spirituality and bring forth into your life greater peace of mind, love, joy, understanding, wisdom, financial prosperity, and your heart's desire. As a spiritual being, all of these things are your spiritual birthright to enjoy on planet Earth. But first you must recognize and realize that there is a real spiritual part of you waiting to unfold within you.

When you need inspiration, need to be uplifted, or need to be more spiritually focused, just flip through these pages and randomly select an affirmation. You may want to dwell upon the thoughts in one affirmation a day or longer, or read several at one time. Carry this book with you in your pocket, purse, or car; place it at your bedside for reading before falling asleep; or put it any place where you can pull it out when you need that spiritual lift or an understanding of something that may be going on around or within you. *Pocket Prayers* is the ideal book to read with the family at night before going to bed. *Pocket Prayers* is a great gift to young adults going off on their own as well as a great gift for family members and friends.

Throughout this book I use the terms *God*, *Creator*, and the *universe* interchangeably. The term *God* is used to personalize our relationship with the universe.

I believe that regardless of our culture, race, or religion, we are all connected by and one with the same spiritual energy force of the universe. Our differences are just the different paths our souls have chosen for us to grow.

Our experience on planet Earth requires us to nourish our minds, bodies, and spirits. We strengthen our bodies by working out and eating healthy. We expand our minds by studying and learning. It is also important to refresh our spirits by giving attention to who we really are and nourishing our spirits. We nourish our spirits by meditating and asking our Creator for daily guidance and direction as we make decisions in our daily living. Realizing that there is something greater than oneself is the first step.

Mediation is the most powerful form of contact you can make with your indwelling Creator. During meditation you may feel nothing is happening; however, you will discover during the course of your daily experiences that answers and solutions will appear before you in the most normal ways. Previous situations that may have been challenging will amaze you by working themselves out.

Jesus Christ and many other modern day spiritual souls have given us all the practical instructions that we need for productive and wonderful daily living. However, we must meditate upon these instructions and take them seriously in order for them to make a positive difference in our lives.

One of the most important principles is the *power of the spoken word*. We spend most of our waking hours talking. Jesus told us that mankind shall not live by bread alone, but by every word that is spoken. Think about all the things that you say during the course of the day. In your speaking, you are affirming *who you are; the direction your life is going; how you feel today; how you will feel tomorrow; what will happen to you, your children, and your family; and your relationship with your friends, coworkers, family, and country*. Sit back and just think about all the things that you are speaking and professing. Are you really aware of what you are speaking and how your spoken word is creating your life? Are all of these words about things that you desire in your life or things that you do not desire in your life?

Your thoughts and words are the driver of your life. Your thoughts and words have *power*. Your thoughts and words are your power; your thoughts and words are the gasoline that drives your life. How are you using your *power?* Are you using the power of your words to create love, happiness, joy, forgiveness, prosperity, and peacefulness in your life? *Thoughts are things*. You can change your life by changing the way you think and what you think about.

We pick up phases that we use in daily living from others. We pick them up from our families, coworkers, friends, TV, songs we sing, music on the radio, etc.

The evidence of this principle is all around you. You can do several experiments aside from looking at your own life. Turn on the TV and watch a movie—the words of the actors shape the plot. Listen to people around you; hear what they are saying and see how those words come to fruition in their lives. The principle is working all around you and with you—just pay attention. Nothing happens by accident; *it is all our planning and design.* God has given us free will, and we must learn to use our free will to our advantage, not disadvantage. We must *wake up* spiritually.

You can change your life by changing your thinking. The first step is to make a conscious decision to make a positive change in your life. *Seriously desire it.* Remember, when you declare to make a positive change in your life that is a *thought.* Remember that *your thoughts form the things, situations, and circumstances that you desire.* Just that one thought has power. Affirm now out loud: *I desire to make positive changes in my life.* Now, if you just say "change," change can take various forms, and it may be a change that you do not desire. Positive change is your key. What you profess you will realize. For example, you may want to go to school to be something you always wanted to be, or maybe you want to open a business, or marry your soul mate, or become more spiritual, or have wellness. Thinking that you can't will bring negative results. Thinking you can will bring positive results. Just as you learned to ride a bicycle with practice, you learn to think in the positive realm by practice. You can gather positive thoughts also by reading positive self-help spiritual books or listening to positive self-help spiritual CDs. Practice listening to positive self-help spiritual CDs while driving your car, doing chores around the house, or before falling asleep at night. Saturating your mind with these truths helps to reinforce your new belief system about yourself. Remember, you are saturating your mind with something; let it be something that is really benefiting you and your life. There are many positive spiritual giants today from which you can learn and grow.

Next you need to set aside some time each day when you can think about the change that you desire in your life. In your daily meditation, ask for guidance and wisdom to affect this change. Write about what it will be like when you have this positive change in your life. Writing or journaling helps you to clarify and put the specifics in your desires. Visualize this positive change. Let the universe determine *how it will happen*. For example, if you desire a certain amount of money, let the universe determine the best way for it to come to you. You make the request, focus on the end result, let the universal force, God, your Creator (whatever you'd like to call it) handle the details. Ask that things happen for you in a happy way, a good way.

The universe has infinite wonderful ways to bless you. You may not be aware of all the wonderful and happy ways that you can be blessed. Infinite intelligence can bring forth your desires in ways you may have never imagined. You may get an idea to go somewhere you have never gone before, do something you have never done before, so follow your hunches. This may be your Creator guiding you to your desired results. Trust your inner guidance. Trust your intuition.

Lastly, you must take action. When you are prompted to do something, go somewhere, or call someone, *do it.* Your Creator is all-knowing and knows exactly how to guide you to your heart's desire. Trust it. You are not alone. That which created you has always been there with you, guiding you to this day, this book, and these instructions, just as I have been guided to write this book for you. The universal power knows exactly how to do everything and how to do it *perfectly.* You are in partnership with the universal power.

If nothing seems to be happening in the beginning, that just means things are being set up; people, situations, and circumstances are being put in place for your desire to manifest.

Much earlier in my life, I desired to meet a companion. After learning the technique of writing down my desires, I began to focus daily on the type of relationship that I wanted to experience. I included the qualities that I would like for him to have— loyal, faithful, loving, kind, etc. I consciously focused on attracting a companion every single day. After about three weeks, a girlfriend called and invited me to a party. Initially I turned down the invitation, but after her persistence, I agreed to go. Upon arriving, a young man entered the room, and we were immediately attracted to each other. We enjoyed a long, loving relationship for years. Call it affirmations, prayer, or whatever your choice of words might be, focusing on your desire is using your God-given power to demonstrate and manifest your desires. Over the years, I have continued to study spirituality and use these principles in my life. My life is filled with answered prayers. It is now that I have been guided to share with you in this book my *pocket prayers*.

Always keep your faith. *Believe.* You will attract all the right people at the right time to manifest your desire. *Keep the faith.* Keep the faith in your Creator. Believe it knows what it is doing, just as a tiny seed can produce a beautiful flower or tall tree with the proper amount of sunshine and water. Your words are your seeds to your future. The tiny seed has in it all the ingredients to make the bark and the leaves of the tree; you too have all the ingredients in your words to attract your heart's desire.

Following are some prayers to help you along your spiritual journey. May your life transform into a marvelous adventure on planet Earth.

MY SPIRITUAL GROWTH

T oday I choose to begin my spiritual growth. I know that which has created me is within me, and it now guides me to my highest good. I know that there is a divine plan for my life. The divine plan for my life includes happiness for me, peace of mind for me, perfect health for me, financial fulfillment for me, and more good than I can imagine.

I realize that I can make choices for my life. I ask my Creator to guide me to make the right and appropriate choices, choices that produce my happiness, peace of mind, perfect health, financial well-being, and fulfillment in every aspect of my life.

Today I call forth the divine plan for my life; today I cooperate with the divine plan for my life; and today I accept the divine plan for my life. As I am given new ideas, I act upon these ideas, making wise choices. Today I realize that everything that I am guided to do is a part of the unfoldment of my divine plan, even if I do not recognize it to be so. I know that my Creator can do for me what it can do through me. I cooperate with the divine process that is unfolding, the divine plan for my life.

I now relax and know that the creative power of the universe that created me is working through me bringing about my heart's desire. As opportunities come before me, I recognize them and take appropriate action. I move forward into greater good in my life.

I now realize that life is a journey, and each opportunity is not the destination, but a part of my journey in life.

AFFIRMATION

I shall keep my faith strong in the universal power working within me and know that everything is working for my highest good.

MY SPIRITUAL AWARENESS

The way I increase my knowledge is to study, read, and listen to others with wisdom. The way I learn to drive a car is to practice driving. The way I learn to swim is by practice. The way I grow spiritually is to learn what spirituality is about and to practice and have spiritual experiences. In the most recent decades, increased attention has been given to our spirituality, what it is, and the role that it plays in mankind's daily living.

The egg and the sperm that was the beginning of my human growth process were created by something greater than my wonderful parents. It is that Creator that created me that I trust to guide me and place opportunities before me. My Creator, which is God, has created me and given me full power to enjoy this earthly experience. I now tap into that power within me during my daily meditations and discover who I really am.

My first step in my spiritual growth and awareness is to know who I am. This process involves redefining myself. As I mediate daily, I realize that I am a spiritual being having a human experience. As a spiritual being, I believe that God created me to thrive as I learn and grow during my earthly experience. As I daily mediate, I become increasingly aware that I have great powers within me to accomplish my goals with amazing success. As I develop my "I can" attitude, I develop the ability to attract the right people, situations, and circumstances that help me accomplish my goals. I am blessed with great opportunities that lead me to success after success. Each success is a stepping stone in my journey to greater success.

As a spiritual being, I am aware that a part of my journey is to help others to realize their spirituality. I inspire and encourage others. I remind others that they can realize their dreams by believing that they can, and they have been endowed with the power to do so.

AFFIRMATION

Every day and in every way I am becoming more aware of my spirituality. Answers now come easily to me as I look to my Creator to guide me. Answers sometimes come through my personal inspirations, people, situations, circumstances, and in ways that I had not expected. I now rejoice in my awareness of my spirituality.

MY THOUGHTS AND WORDS

I know that which has created me works through my thoughts and words to create my life. Today I chose to think the very best and the most positive thoughts for my life, my world, and all of my affairs. I know that my thoughts manifest into things. I am careful with the thoughts that I choose to think and the words that I choose to speak about myself and others.

I know that the spiritual principal "The power of my word" that Jesus used and talked about works in my life too. I know that when I say that I can't, circumstances set up in such a way that makes things difficult for me. I also know as I speak words "I can" or "I will," the same principle works for me and creates opportunities for me to accomplish my goal. This principle does not know hard or easy, it *only works*. When someone says to me, "Have a good day," I respond by saying, "I will, and you have a good day too."

Daily, I incorporate more positive thoughts, which now become my new belief system. I now attract into my life positive-thinking people who inspire me with their positive thoughts. I too am an inspiration to others. I now read books that promote my positive thinking. I watch positive, inspiring movies and TV shows that inspire me.

I know that which has created me is now guiding me to be the very best that I can be. My life is unfolding beautifully. I am thankful to know and realize the principle of the power of my word, and I thank my Creator for setting things up this way and my realization of it. Every day in every way things are getting better and better for me.

I imagine there is a little guardian angel sitting on my shoulder reminding me to think and speak only positive thoughts and words about myself and others.

I now chose thoughts that give me *peace of mind*. I do not allow thoughts of anger, hate, jealousy, fear, and unforgiveness steal my peace of mind. My little guardian angel reminds me of negative thoughts that enter my mind, and I send those negative thoughts into the sea of nothingness. I repeat this process as many times as necessary until it is uprooted from my thinking.

I recognize that negative thoughts give me an uneasy feeling. I now realize that I can change how I feel by changing the thoughts that I choose to think. When negative thoughts appear, I immediately transform that thought to a positive thought. I replace negative thoughts with thoughts of love, kindness, forgiveness, understanding, and peace. As I practice replacing negative thoughts with positive ones, I feel a deep sense of peace within myself.

As I transform my thinking, I realize there is good in every situation and in every person. I look for the good. I find the good in situations and people. Each transformed thought empowers me to be a more peaceful, successful, and happy person.

AFFIRMATION

My word is my tool to navigate through life. I chose my words carefully. I speak of what I desire and not of what I do not desire. I now realize that God and the universal law of my spoken word, which He has given me to live under, allows for the perfect outworking of any situation. I now rejoice in knowing this truth.

MY ATTITUDE

My attitude is always a reflection of what I am thinking. If I am thinking negative thoughts about myself, I feel sad about myself. If I am thinking negatively about someone, I feel sad about him or her. Negative attitudes are supported by feelings of hurt, jealousy, disappointment, and anger. I remember that all the thoughts that I think I have chosen to accept as my own. These thoughts make up my attitude. I adopt attitudes from my environment, family, friends, television, radio, coworkers, books, and sometimes strangers. I have the choice to determine which thoughts I want to adopt as my own. There are thoughts that make me feel happy, sad, joyous, faith-filled, healthy, disappointed, angry, thankful, or sick. I can choose the thoughts that I think, thus choosing my attitude.

Environment plays an important role in my attitude. The people I am around influence my attitude either in a positive or negative way. In turn, I can also influence the attitudes of the people around me. I now chose to be around positive thinking and positive feeling people. This reinforces my positive feelings and beliefs.

I start today to consciously choose thoughts about myself and others that are positive up lifting thoughts. I start today to develop a positive attitude about myself and others. Instead of being critical about myself and others, I find things to praise and complement about myself and others. Instead of feeling lonely or depressed, I decide to find something that I enjoy doing, and I do it. I look at my life and look at ways to improve my attitude about myself and others. There is always something good that I can say or think about myself or others to make me or them feel good. Feeling good about things and people makes me have a good attitude about myself and others.

I now decide to look at the bright side of life. There are so many wonderful things about life that makes me feel cheerful, happy, and thankful. I keep a check on my attitude about myself. I am a wonderful creation of God equipped with amazing talents and abilities that I am using and discovering. I keep a check on my attitude in my relationships with others. When I awake in the morning, I start my day off being thankful for all that I have and all that I am. I make sure as I meet others that I find some way to compliment them.

AFFIRMATION

I now cleanse myself of negative thoughts and feelings about myself and others. I now replace negative thoughts and feelings with positive thoughts and feelings of love, kindness, hope, and encouragement. I keep a positive attitude about myself and others. My life is transformed and empowered with the transformation of my attitude.

MY CHALLENGES

---◆-❁-◆---

My challenges are simply opportunities to grow and move forward with my life. When a challenge appears, I do not dwell upon it; I simply look to God to assist me by providing the people, circumstances, and resources I need to easily and peacefully resolve the situation and move forward. There is nothing too hard for God to do. God is all-knowing and all-capable to assist me in any situation. I give thanks for this insight, this *truth* in my daily living. If I spend time dwelling upon a challenge, I empower it. I stop and remember to keep my thoughts on the power of God within me to overcome any situation.

As I look back on my old way of thinking, I understand clearly now why my life was going the way that it was going. My previous negative way of thinking was manifesting negative situations for me. Realizing this truth, I now change my thinking to positive, happy, healthy thoughts. I now let go of old, worn out ways of thinking and think of new ideas that propel me to my heart's desire.

I meditate daily on things that are beautiful, good, happy, and wholesome. I surround myself with positive-thinking people. I realize that my old way of thinking was learned over the years, so I am patient with myself as I adopt my new way of thinking. I know that as I persist in making this change, challenges now become opportunities for me to grow.

I look forward to good and great things happening to me. I welcome blessings to flow in my life.

I give thanks for the blessings that I presently enjoy in my life and the blessings that are forthcoming. I walk around my house and give thanks for everything in it. If my health has been a challenge, I now give thanks daily for my body. I daily bless my body, my muscles, organs, nerves, tissues, and the cells in my body.

If relationships have been a challenge in my past, I now give thanks to the people in my life. I tell them that I love and appreciate them. If at first it is hard to find something to compliment them on, I start with little things that I appreciate about them. As I look for good in others, I find good in others.

AFFIRMATION

Challenges are opportunities for me to grow. I am strengthened by these opportunities. I now understand that there are answers to all challenges. I believe that God has equipped me with all that I need to live a rich and fulfilling life. I now move forward to the fulfillment of this blessing.

MY FAITH

hen I have faith in something, I believe in something that does not yet exist. Therefore *faith* is belief in the unseen—belief in something that has not yet happened or manifested. I have faith in many things, faith that I will rise in the morning, get dressed, prepare and eat breakfast, drive to work, or go about my daily activities. Because this is something that I do daily or is a part of my routine, I think very little about it; I just go through the action of doing it. Yet I am using *faith*. I *believe* that I am going to do those things, and I just automatically do them.

Let's say for example that I decide that I would like a better job, or marriage and a family, to write and publish a book, or run a business of my own. To do this, I apply my *faith*—faith that I *can* do this. I now believe in the not-yet-manifested. The first thing that I do is to plan and visualize my goal. I do this in detail. I may journal about this dream. This may take some time, just depending on the amount of detail and energy I put into it. I see myself already there, or the goal already manifested. I may then get a telephone call or a hunch or an opportunity to go somewhere, or read something in the newspaper or on the Internet that guides me to my destination. This is the action part. Next is the manifestation. Now let's look at what is really happening. During my prayerful process, I am forming in my mind the answer that I desire, always including the idea of this or something better. Forming the idea in my mind helps me recognize it when it manifests. The universe knows all and is in all and knows exactly what is best for me. The universe knows what is for my highest good. To this extent, I let go of my desire for the universe to manifest my desire perfectly. I allow for the universe to include things that I may have omitted but are best for me.

My *faith* and *belief* that I can have my desire makes me a magnet to the thing or situation desired. I am the one that is just simply making a request, a prayer, expressing a desire. It is the universal power or God that sets up situations and circumstances to bring it to me. Knowing that I am in partnership with God and universal powers make me humble and thankful for my desired results. My faith is that the wonderful loving presence of God helps me to accomplish my desires. My faith is a vital part of the process of my prayers being answered. *Faith* is the part that I play in the manifestation of my desires. When it is time, I will be guided to take the proper action for the manifestation.

AFFIRMATION

I have *faith* in God to guide and direct my path to the fulfillment of my desires.

MY PATIENCE

When I think of patience, I think it's time for me to wait. Patience is a time for me to have faith and know that dreams, goals, and aspirations are working out for me, even though I may not see any evidence of things at work. When a seed is planted in the ground, it must be nourished by the rain and sunshine in order to grow. My patience is the sunshine and rain nourishing my desire, dream, or goal.

I do not sit and watch a flower grow; that would be tiring and stressful. So, after forming my dream, desire, or goal, I water it with my faith and use this time to prepare for the end results. If it is a soul mate partner that I am praying for, I use this time to imagine the harmony, love, cooperation, understanding, and joy that I will experience in this relationship. I may do this by absorbing the positive energy from loving couples that I know or by watching loving, happy-ending movies. All of this prepares me for my experience of having a loving, lasting relationship. This is the rain and sunshine that I give to my desire.

If it is a career or job that I am seeking, I use the same principles that nature has shown me to nurture my desire. I form in my mind the type of work that I would like to do. It will be a job in which I am able to use my natural talents and God-given abilities, working with people whom I enjoy in a perfect location for me, a job that is completely fulfilling to me in every way. I make this my main focus. I move away from anything or anyone that is contradictory to my desire.

I wait patiently for the opportunity that guides me to the unfolding of my desire. As co-creator with the divine energy of the universe, I believe that my desire is forming from my thoughts, feelings, and words. I make sure that all my words, thoughts, and feelings are positive about my desire. If I begin to doubt or feel fearful or depressed as to whether my desire will manifest, I immediately turn my attention to a happy thing, feeling, or experience that I have had in the past and know that the universe is forming the manifestation of my desire. The universe is bringing all the right people and situations to me. I am patient.

AFFIRMATION

I am patient with myself. I wait for the universe to bring everything and everyone in place for the manifestation of my heart's desire.

MY PRAYERS

———— • ❀ • ————

Prayer is a request for something or a set of circumstances. I realize that I am asking God, the universal power that flows through me as it flows through everything. I now examine my definition of who God is to me. I now realize that it is not a man in the sky, but a force, a power, a law that operates for me. God is not someone or something that might give this desire to me if I am good or deserving. God is a force that watches over me, provides for me, and protects me through various channels (people, situations, circumstances) as I ask and believe. God is really something that I really can't imagine, but I can define my relationship to God and how God operates in my life. God does not hold back any desire that I may have; I do that when I give in to doubt and fear. God is always ready, willing, and able to supply all of my needs.

When I pray, I believe that God can answer my prayers. The more I pray and receive answered prayers, the more established my relationship with God becomes. It is the same as how I establish a relationship with a friend. The more time we spend together, the more we get to know each other and trust each other, the better our relationship becomes.

There is nothing that God can't do for me. I now expand my definition of God to embrace this greatness. God can remove obstacles that I have tried for a lifetime to remove. God can do for me what I can't do for myself. God can do for me that which I believe He can do. If I believe God can, God will. God can do for me what He can do *through me*. God works through people, events, circumstances, and situations to bring my desire to me. These are the channels through which God quietly works.

I now develop a partnership with God. My relationship with God grows as I watch His works in my life and the life of others. There is nothing too great for God to do for me. As my blessings flow into my life and are received with thankfulness, my relationship with God is strengthened.

AFFIRMATION

I can do nothing; God does the work, and I am thankful.

MY AFFIRMATIONS

————•—✹—•————

W
e are constantly affirming. We are constantly speaking that which we desire and do not desire. We are constantly forming our worlds with our words. We are creative beings creating our todays, tomorrows, and our futures with our thoughts and spoken words. We either speak words for ourselves or someone speaks words for us that we accept as our own.

Affirmations are ways in which we use our God-given power to reinforce and change our thought patterns. Affirmations are a way of changing your life circumstances. If you desire to lose weight, you find a weight loss program. This program teaches you new ideas, new foods to eat, and what those foods will do for you, or you start an exercise program for weight loss. All these life-altering opportunities teach you a new way of thinking. Thus, it is your thinking that drives your life. It is your thinking that drives your change.

Knowing this principle of life, I now affirm and begin my journey of adopting positive thoughts about all areas of my life. In doing so, I accept a partnership with my indwelling

God to guide me to a deeper understanding of how to make positive changes in my life. I now let go of negative thoughts and feelings about myself and others and replace them with positive thoughts and feelings about myself and others. I now accept that my affirmations are of things in life that I choose. I now deny and cancel all negative thoughts and feelings about myself and others.

I now train myself to think the highest thoughts, and with practice I am able to transform my life, conditions, and circumstances into very desirable and happy conditions and circumstances. I now thank God for this new idea of affirmations.

AFFIRMATION

I now affirm only the very positive for my life and others.

MY AGING

W hether I am twenty years old or sixty years old, my physical body is aging. Aging does not mean deteriorating. Aging is just a measurement of the time that my body is on Earth. As I enjoy birthday after birthday, I remain mindful of maintaining my body's health. I realize that my body is the vehicle that carries me about my daily activities. I love my body. I take care of my body with good nutrition and exercise.

One of the keys to keeping a strong, healthy body is the movement of all of my body parts. I am now conscious of how important it is to stay active and fit. As I age, I am conscious of daily exercising my arms, fingers, legs, knees, toes, torso, neck, head, and all of my body parts. My body was created to move. If I enjoy exercising with others, I join a fitness club. If I am self-motivated, I develop an exercise routine at home. I do whatever works for me to keep a fit, active, and healthy body.

With my new exercise program, I feel great every day. I feel a positive difference in my body and body movements. My body is flexible; my body is strong. I am energetic as I go about my daily activities.

As my body ages, I age gracefully. I continue with my daily exercises well into my senior years. I am able to do all the activities that I enjoy effortlessly. I remain conscious of staying active. I am thankful for the idea of being active. My senior years are my best years.

AFFIRMATION

I age gracefully. I enjoy my daily exercise program, and I feel great. My body is flexible, strong, and healthy.

MY MANIFESTATIONS

————•◉•————

Manifestations are things, situations, circumstances, events, or people that I would like to have in my life. I visualize, think upon, pray about, and meditate on that which I desire until I feel very comfortable with my desire. If it is a job or business idea, I get very specific in my mind and thoughts about it. I visualize myself doing or being this new manifestation in my life.

As I look to God to guide me in my life to achieve this goal or have this manifestation which I desire, I realize that my answers, the directions that I am to take, can come to me in infinite ways. My answers can come during my quite meditations, from a friend or family member, from a television program, from something I read in a book or on the Internet, or from a stranger. There are infinite ways that my answers can come to me.

I know that I am working with infinite intelligence to bring this desire into my life. If I am to take steps or do any particular thing to prepare myself, I do it with excitement and enthusiasm, knowing that I am being divinely guided. As I

23

patiently and excitedly wait for directions on what to do, where to go, or who to call, I have complete faith in its fulfillment. I know that my belief in God's provision for me is certain and sure. I do not allow anyone or anything to deter me from my good. Everything and everyone is supportive of me in the fulfillment of my desire.

Before my desire appears, I give thanks to God for its fulfillment. As I think upon my fulfilled desire, I am filled with gratitude and thanksgiving. I know that my fulfilled desire is a blessing to me and a blessing to others.

AFFIRMATION

I give thanks to God for all the blessings that I have and those I expect to have in my life, my world, and in all of my affairs.

MY PEACE OF MIND

————————•◉•————————

I now choose thoughts that give me peace of mind. Peace of mind is a feeling that everything is alright. Everything is in divine order. I know that my Creator has charge over everything, and I work in partnership with my Creator.

My experience on Earth is like a school. It's a place for us humans to learn, grow, and express more God-like qualities. Knowing that all is in the process of growth and becoming gives me peace of mind. Knowing that something greater than me, greater than us, is in charge, gives me peace of mind. Knowing that everything happens for a reason gives me peace; even if I do not know the purpose right away, I know it will unfold. Knowing that the Earth is a playground for me to learn and grow gives me peace of mind. It is a place for me to realize that I am a part of my Creator. How could I be anything else? I look back at how mankind has advanced over the ages and is still growing, and this gives me peace of mind.

As I change my perspective of the world and my world, I become more peaceful. As I pray for increased understanding and divine protection, I become more peaceful. As I realize that God watches over me as He does everyone and everything, I become more peaceful. As I become more peaceful, everything and everyone in my life becomes more peaceful. I now know that as I become more peaceful, God is using me to help others around me to become more peaceful; they feel my peacefulness. I radiate peace. I am open and receptive to God showering peace of mind in my life, my world, and in all of my affairs. I am a channel through which God showers peace of mind on others.

I now make a conscious decision when something happens not quite in the way that I planned to stop and know that this must be a part of the process of something bigger and better for me.

I keep my peace of mind. I know there is good in everything and that everything is just a stepping stone to something greater.

If someone says or does something that I do not agree with, I know they are saying or doing it from their consciousness, and it has nothing to do with me. I keep my peace of mind even when I do not agree with others.

I remain at peace with a clear mind regardless of what is going on around me. I do not let others steal my peace of mind. My new understanding gives me peace of mind. I am thankful for my peace of mind. I celebrate my peace of mind.

As I become more peaceful, others are affected by my peace, and this calms situations. As I practice my peace of mind, I am able to remain peaceful in all situations.

As I meditate on peace of mind daily, I become a more peaceful person. As I think about my life, I know that I am doing exactly what I need to be doing right now, and I am at peace. As I look to my future, I know that God has wonderful blessings for me. I give thanks for the blessings that I now enjoy regardless of how great or small, and this thought gives me peace.

I enjoy fun, happy, and peaceful relationships with my friends. My friends are blessings to me, and I am a blessing to my friends.

I now chose thoughts that give me *peace of mind*. I do not allow thoughts of anger, hate, jealousy, fear, and unforgiveness rob me of my peace of mind.

I recognize that negative thoughts give me an uneasy feeling. I now realize that I can change how I feel by changing the thoughts that I choose to think. When a negative thought appears, I immediately transform that thought to its opposite. I replace negative thoughts with thoughts of love, kindness, understanding, and peace. As I practice replacing negative thoughts with positive ones, I feel a deep sense of peace within myself.

As I transform my thinking, I realize that there is good in every situation and in every person. I look for the good. I find the good in situations and people. Each of my transformed thoughts empowers me to be a more peaceful person.

My peace of mind is important to me. I do not allow others to steal my peace of mind. I am peaceful and happy.

AFFIRMATION

I enjoy peace of mind in my life because I have a new understanding of life. I choose peace of mind in all of my experiences. I let the peace that goes beyond all understanding dwell within me because I know God is in charge of all things. I trust in God for the perfect solutions to all situations in the world and in my personal world. My faith is strong.

MY RELATIONSHIPS

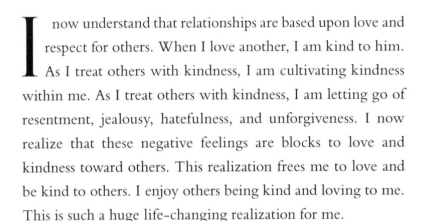

I now understand that relationships are based upon love and respect for others. When I love another, I am kind to him. As I treat others with kindness, I am cultivating kindness within me. As I treat others with kindness, I am letting go of resentment, jealousy, hatefulness, and unforgiveness. I now realize that these negative feelings are blocks to love and kindness toward others. This realization frees me to love and be kind to others. I enjoy others being kind and loving to me. This is such a huge life-changing realization for me.

I give out what I want to receive.

I now enjoy happy, loving, wholesome, and fulfilling relationships with others. My life is filled with wonderful, loving family and friends. I am loving and kind to them, and I receive loving kindness in return.

Respect is being okay when someone thinks differently from me. I live and let live. When others have beliefs that are different than mine, I respect their beliefs. I no longer argue about our differences. I simply recognize their beliefs as a part of their journeys in life. This helps me to keep peace in my relationships. As we discuss various issues, I respect others' opinions and share my opinions in a kind and diplomatic manner in order for us to have peace in our relationships. I realize differences contribute to our growth. A difference is simply a new idea presented to another. Either we think about it and grow from it or discard it. With this method I can keep peace in my relationships.

Peace and harmony are my relationship goals. I now attract friends and family members that share like relationship goals.

I enjoy loving and lasting relationships with those who share the same relationship goals. Like attracts like. This principle works beautifully in my life now.

AFFIRMATION

I now enjoy fulfilling relationships with others.

I live and let live. My new understanding helps me to keep my peace of mind and peace in my relationships.

MY FAMILY

——◦—◦—❋—◦—◦——

M
y family is God's blessing to me. We are joined together because of the lessons we are to learn and the qualities we are to develop. Some of the life lessons are to be more loving, to be more forgiving, to learn respect for others, to share, to become wiser, to be more understanding, to receive encouragement, and to become more confident. All of these qualities build character.

I am thankful for my family. My family and I have a special bond. Our bond is a lifelong bond. My family is the baseline for my growth. I learn from my family members, and my family members learn from me. As I grow, I may change my ideas and ideals, but I thank my Creator that my family is the baseline for my growth.

As I move forward in life, marry and have children, I remain close to my family and build my own family. I use the same positive principles of life to teach my family. We respect and love each other.

As we build families generation after generation, we build upon stronger bonds of love and helpfulness with one another.

This teaches me to go into the world with the same ideas and ideals to share with others. These principles help me to be successful in life.

I love and appreciate my family.

AFFIRMATION

I love and appreciate my family. My family is the baseline for who I define myself to be today. I thank God for giving me my family.

MY PARTNER

---◆·❀·◆---

To walk through life with a soulmate partner is a blessing. To share life and life's experiences with someone whom I love unconditionally and who loves me unconditionally and is supportive of my efforts eases the challenges in life and elevates the joyous times in life.

My partner is a gift from God to me. My partner and I share the same values of loyalty to each other, trust and respect for each other, and kindness toward each other, all of which make up our loving relationship. We are compassionate and understanding of each other.

My partner is my friend that I can always depend; my partner is my family-building partner. My partner is my lover; my partner is my confidant; my partner is my gift from God.

My partner and I share the same ideals, morals, and beliefs in God. This allows us to enjoy a life-long harmonious relationship and marriage. When we have a difference of opinion about a situation, we respect the other's opinion, express our opinions, and come to a meeting of the minds with each other either then or later. We find it is more important to be happy that to be right. Our differences complement each other and help us grow. The most important thing to us both is our love for each other. We do not allow a difference in opinion to separate us.

My partner is a good parent to our children. We not only teach our children good values, we show them in our daily living. We believe it is important to respect others whether you are at the grocery store or in a corporate meeting. We believe, live, and teach being kind and helpful to others. We consider how our words and actions make others feel.

My partner and I laugh and have fun together. We enjoy each other's company. We enjoy the company of friends that share our values and beliefs.

I appreciate my partner and feel very blessed that I do not have to live life alone. I tell my partner often how appreciative I am for the love and tolerance shown toward my flaws. I also communicate that I love how my good qualities are appreciated and noticed. I know that God provided me with this wonderful partner, and I thank God often for this blessing. My partner is like a piece of God in my life, and I am like a piece of God in their life.

My life partner and I enjoy the same type of activities and social and spiritual events. We share many common interests and enjoy spending time with each other. We are the most important people to each other.

I always consider my partner before making important decisions. My important decisions not only affect my life, but also my partner's life. As we discuss important decisions, my partner many times makes me aware of aspects that I had previously not considered. Our minds working together always bring good results. Working out situations together reinforces our loving partnership. Our decisions always yield results that are pleasurable to us both. We are faithful and loyal to each other. We are honest with each other.

We touch, hug, and kiss each other often. Coming together with a touch, hug, or kiss always ignites a warm spark of our unity, love, and devotion to one another.

AFFIRMATION

I feel so blessed to have and enjoy the companionship of my partner. My partner is like a piece of God in my life. I am like a piece of God in my partner's life.

MY CHILDREN

———— • ❀ • ————

y children are a way in which God blesses my life. When my children entered my life, it was like God gave me an incarnated part of itself. My children opened me up to express one of my God-like qualities— unconditional love. Unconditional love has no boundaries. Unconditional love is all-protecting. Unconditional love is self-sacrificing. Unconditional love knows no fear. Unconditional love conquers all. Unconditional love is selfless. Unconditional love is all-embracing. Unconditional love is greater than any emotion on Earth. It is with the unconditional love that I feel and express to my children that I fully realize God's love for me.

I am a part of God. My children are a part of God. As a parent, I am a caretaker of a part of God. As a caretaker of my children, I equip them with life skills. I teach them kindness, respect, confidence, responsibility, loving others, and being the best that they can be.

Not only do I teach my children, but my children are my teachers. My children remind me to be loving and supportive when their choices are different from the choices I would have made for them. My children remind me that now that I have equipped them with the basics of life, their journeys may be different from my journey. This teaches me to respect my children's inner divine guidance. Each life has a divine purpose in the total scheme of things. I therefore rely on God's divine plan for my children.

I am proud of my children. I am proud of who they have become. I am proud of their accomplishments, which are making the world a better place for us all.

AFFIRMATION

God gives me my children whether they come through me or to me. I love my children continuously with the same unconditional love that God loves me.

MY FRIENDS

———•❖•———

M y friends are as welcome as sunshine in my life. A friend is always someone with whom you share common beliefs, interest, ideas, ideals, hopes, and dreams. A friend is someone that you love, trust, confide in, and feel safe with. He or she is someone who is faithful and loyal to you, and whose company you enjoy.

My friends are blessings to me. I am a blessing to my friends. My friends are supportive of me in the things that I do and the things that I hope to do. I am always supportive of my friends. I can always depend on my friends to encourage me during difficult or challenging times. This makes my friends a blessing from God to me. My friends are a safety net for me when I need help. This mutual exchange of kindness is the bond that binds our friendship.

There are those friends that are friends for a lifetime, and there are those that are friends for a season or more. God knows my needs and provides the temporary or lifelong friends to me. Whether my friends are lifelong or seasonal, I value and appreciate all of my friends.

If I move to a new location, God blesses me with new friends. It is so amazing to me that my friends are also looking for a new friend like me. We find each other. I am always attracting genuine friends that I trust. This makes me feel safe with my friends.

AFFIRMATION

I value and appreciate my God sent friends.

MY COMPASSION

———•◦❀◦•———

When I think of compassion, I think of how human beings are so much alike. We all have the same basic needs of food, water, and shelter. I also think that we all have a need to be loved, the need to feel safe, the need for wellness, and the need to feel that others care about us.

I show my compassion to others by being conscious of their needs and supportive of them if they are going through a challenge. I give them love and encouragement. In turn, others give me love and encouragement if I am having a challenge in my life. I am aware that I may receive compassion from someone different than the one to whom I was compassionate. The one to whom I was compassionate may not be the one to return compassion to me. God knows my needs and always places the right people in my life to show compassion to me. It is important for me to realize that I don't give to a person to get something back. I give because I am guided to give. I now let the universe determine the best source from which I receive my blessing.

I am nourished by the compassion of family, friends, and associates. It is the ways in which God satisfies my basic need to be loved and cared for. All of this giving to me makes me feel whole and complete. All of this giving makes me feel a responsibility to return the giving in ways that I am guided to do so.

I now do unto others the good that has been done unto me and more. All the love and good deeds that have nourished me I now return to others. I now recognize that the basic needs that I have are the same basic needs that others have. Compassion for others is now born within me. As this compassion awakens within me, I feel a deep desire to be helpful and kind to those that I am guided to help. As I exercise more and more compassion toward others, my ability to help others grows and expands. My compassion might extend to a family member, a friend, a coworker, an associate, or a country. I stand ready to help.

AFFIRMATION

Compassion for others is now born within me.

MY SELF-LOVE

———•✤•———

To love oneself is to realize self-love. Not the self that others think of you being, but how you define yourself. I now know that I have the choice to define who I am in the way that I choose. I now define myself in the highest ways that I can conceive, and I work each day to become my own self-definition.

I define myself in a self-accepting way, and I focus on my strengths, not my faults. I am loving and kind to myself and others. I find kind things to do for others, and I am confident in the things that I do. I think before I do and say things, which lets the wisdom within me spring forth. I am wise, I am happy. I find opportunities to smile and laugh when I am alone and when I am with others. I find things that I enjoy doing alone, such as reading, writing or journaling, sitting quietly praying, meditating, or just thinking about things that make me happy. I am healthy, and I enjoy cooking and eating healthy foods that nourish my body.

Loving myself means that I feel a deep sense of peace about who I have defined myself to be when I am alone. When I think of my accomplishments large and small, I am thankful for them. When I am with others, I feel strong and confident and radiate love to others.

Loving myself allows me to love others. When I am judgmental of myself, I tend to be judgmental of others. Any negative quality that I put on myself I tend to put on others. I now transform this feeling into feeling positive about myself; I then am able to be more loving and compassionate toward others. As I am more loving, patient, kind, and compassionate to myself, I am more loving, kind, patient, and compassionate toward others. I give out what I want to receive.

As I practice more self-love, I am happier and more at peace with myself. I feel good about myself, where I am in my life, and where I am going.

AFFIRMATION

I love myself. I love who I am. I accept that I can define who I am. I am my best self.

MY CHANGE IN MY LIFE

———— • ✦ • ————

C hange can come into my life in different forms; it could be the loss of a loved one, the loss of a job, a graduation from school, a promotion on my job, a divorce, a new life partner, marriage, change in my health, a healing of my health, moving to a new city, moving into a new home, having a child, or adopting a pet. There are many forms of change that can take place in my life. Some change I am prepared for, and some change can come unexpectedly. Whether change is expected or unexpected, change always moves me forward into new sets of circumstances.

Change is always my teacher. New circumstances may teach me when one opportunity ends, another opportunity can open for me. Change can teach me love, how to be more loving and compassionate toward others, and how to accept love from others. Change can provide me with new skills to use in my career. Change can deepen my understanding of myself and my life. Change can teach me to be more aware of my health and love myself more. Change can bring my heart's desire. Change can bring me peace of mind. Change can bring me increased joy and happiness in my life. Change can make me wiser. Change can bring new friends into my life. Change can improve my financial affairs. Change can give me a new self-image. Change can be very rewarding for me.

Change is the way life unfolds for me. Change is the manifestation of yesterday's dreams and affirmations.

I pray for positive change. I welcome wonderful, happy changes in my life. I enjoy the wonderful unfoldment of the divine plan of my life, which is always welcome change.

AFFIRMATION

I now accept positive and beneficial change in my life that adds to my happiness, peace of mind, good health, and prosperity.

MY CALMNESS

———•━■▶•❋•◀■━•———

I take one step at a time, one day at a time, one activity at a time. I no longer hurry when doing things. I now realize that I have my own rhythm in doing things. Whether I am a fast talker, medium talker, or slow talker, I find my own rhythm. I do not try to imitate others; I find my own rhythm that I am comfortable with and remain there in my talking, walking, and thinking. As I discover my own rhythm in life, I feel calmer and more relaxed within myself. Sometimes this allows for change in the way that I do things. This might mean a different type of work, different friends, or a different lifestyle. I realize that this life is my life; I can create it in the way that suits me best, and I do it in the best way for me. I do not have to imitate others; I can just be myself, and I am now calm.

As I make changes in my life that give me the feeling of calmness, I become more creative. I am now operating from my God-center. I am now more successful in the things that I do. I remain centered and calm and give each activity my full attention. As I calmly practice doing the task before me, I perform with greater effectiveness and efficiency. I am more focused and more successful in the things that I do. I am rewarded in my work and praised by my boss, coworkers, associates, family, and friends as I do the things that are required of me. I am now being my best self.

I radiate calmness, and others around me feel my calmness. I am a role model for others to practice calmness in their lives and daily activities.

I thank God for blessing me with the idea of calmness. My calmness improves my health. My new rhythm removes the stress that I previously felt in my body. My body radiates health. My calmness allows me to put more thought into making healthy food choices, which helps me to establish and maintain my body weight.

I am now doing the things that I enjoy, and I feel great.

AFFIRMATION

I now approach things, people, and situations with calmness. My new rhythm gives me a new sense of well-being and success in my life, my world, and in all of my affairs.

MY STRENGTH

W hen circumstances in life arise that require me to have faith in a positive outcome of a situation, this is when I must put all of my trust and confidence in my Creator. It is a time to let go and let God give me the strength to accept the best outcome of the situation. Sometimes the journey of life can be difficult, and it is in difficult times that I call upon my Creator to give me the strength and faith to see it through.

That strength can come in various ways. It could be remembering a verse from the Bible or quotation from a book or person; it could be the comforting words from a friend; it could be a message on a card; and it could be just a peace that comes over me regarding the situation. Whatever comforts me, I hold on to that and let time reveal the best outcome of the situation.

In difficult times, it is important for me to keep my balance, my emotional, physical, and spiritual balance that can only come from what I think and believe. If my belief system does not include thoughts that comfort me, I call upon the support of others, such as a family member, friend, minister, coworker, or even a stranger. I also find comfort in written literature.

I always remember where there is faith, there is help. Faith is hope in the unseen. Help will come. I accept the form in which help comes to me.

Giving up is never an option. God always responds to me. The only direction that God gives me is forward. I am open and receptive to my help. There is always an answer to every situation that I may have. I maintain my strength, and God sustains me always.

AFFIRMATION

I am now open and receptive to help in my situation. God always answers my prayers. God is my sustaining power by providing me with help that strengthens me.

MY HOME

M y home is not only a physical place where I reside; my home is my place of peace, comfort, and joy. My home is my sanctuary. I am thankful for the house in which I reside, my home. My home is a place where I feel safe and protected. My home is a place where I am at peace and can rejuvenate myself after a busy day. My home is a place of lovingness with my family. My home is a place where I can find rest and relaxation. My home is a place where I entertain my family and friends. My home is a special place for me.

God blesses me with the wisdom, insight, and guidance to sustain and maintain my home. I take care of my home by keeping it clean and comfortable. I am guided by the infinite wisdom within me to make right decisions regarding the maintenance of my home. When I discover things that need to be done, God always provides me with the people and resources to do them. I am thankful for the ability to keep a wonderful home.

I am thankful to have such a wonderful home to enjoy socializing with my family and friends. It is a place where we talk, laugh, and have fun.

I walk through my home daily and give thanks for all of my furnishing and all the items that I have. I give thanks for all that I have and all that I hope to have. I give thanks for my ability to financially maintain and keep my home for as long as I choose.

AFFIRMATION

Thank you, God, for the comfort and enjoyment of my wonderful home.

MY HEALTH

---·•◉•·---

My good health is the single most important part of my life to me. My good health allows me to happily, peacefully, and successfully go about my daily activities. My good health allows me to daily perform my work and easily accomplish the tasks that are placed before me. My good health allows me to care for my family and perform daily chores around my home. My good health allows me to enjoy social activities with my friends and family.

My good health includes my physical, emotional, mental, and spiritual health. I maintain my physical health by making wise food choices and exercising my body daily. My daily physical health promotes the health of my cells, organs, tissues, muscles, and nerves. Knowing that God is always with me and in all of my experiences helps me keep my emotions balanced and calm in various situations. I keep my mind stimulated with positive thoughts and feelings, which promotes my mental health. I read positive books and watch positive, inspirational television programs. My spiritual health is reinforced by my daily affirmations and prayers. My daily mediation and prayers help me to enjoy a positive outlook on my life.

I am thankful for my good health. I am thankful for the ability to do the things that I enjoy. I am thankful for being able to enjoy visiting family members, friends, or a great vacation. My good health allows me to have a great, fulfilling life. I thank God for placing all of the wonderful people and literature in my life to remind me what I need to do to enjoy good health continuously.

I am amazed how my heart beats perfectly without my assistance. I am amazed by my perfect vision, which allows me to see so any beautiful things around me. I am amazed by how I am able to hear the many sounds of nature and the voices of people around me. I am amazed that I can enjoy the smell of many fragrances around me. I am amazed with the perfect operation of the various organs of my body. I am amazed with the ease in which I can move the many parts of my body. My body is a magnificent masterpiece made by my Creator. I never cease to be amazed by the perfection of my body. I give thanks for my body and its perfect health.

AFFIRMATION

Thank you, God, for my continuous good health throughout my long, healthy life.

MY HELPFULNESS TO OTHERS

I now let God use me to help others. I realize that we are all channels through which God blesses. Since God is not in the form of a human being but is within each of us, I now let God use me as a channel through which blessings flow to others. As a channel through which God flows to help others, I am watchful for opportunities to help another. In this like oneness, I am obedient to helping others.

We all have special talents and abilities. Helpfulness to another might be a kind word, a special deed, or a smile. I welcome each morning with a smile and a "Good morning" to my family and a smile and "Good night" before retiring to bed. As I walk through my office, a business, or the mall, I greet others with a kind word or smile.

Kindness to others can be expressed in many ways. Kindness is expressed by holding the door for someone behind me, preparing dinner for an elderly person, providing school supplies for needy children, donating my time money or resources to a homeless shelter, giving genuine service in my business, calling a friend in need of encouragement, cutting my neighbor's grass, writing a book, being a listening ear to a friend, being courteous to the store clerk, or saying a special prayer for a family member, friend, associate, stranger, or the world.

As I realize that we are all connected by the one Spirit of God, I welcome opportunities to help others. Helping others makes me feel good about myself. Helping others is fulfilling to me and helps me to realize my purpose.

AFFIRMATION

I enjoy helping others. Helping others is fulfilling to me.

MY JOY

———•———❁———•———

J oy is the upscale of happiness. Whatever brings me joy
lingers as happiness. I think about the things that bring
me joy. It might be receiving an unexpected large sum of
money, meeting my soul mate, marriage to my soul mate, getting
a new pet, going on an exciting vacation, a career promotion
or a deal coming to a close, a new hobby, volunteering for
an organization, donating money to a worthy cause, being
instrumental in someone's life turning in a positive direction,
good news from my doctor, or a child graduating from school.
There are many things that bring joy to me. I now sit down and
write out ten things that bring me joy. I feel the excitement of
it. Thank you, God, for blessings that bring me joy.

If I do not yet have that joyful thing, event, or person
in my life, I take time each day to feel joy about that thing,
circumstance, or person I anticipate having in my life. I
remember I am the architect of my life. I remember my
words and feelings precede the thing I desire. Create. Create.
Create.

I now choose to have increased joy in my life. I am now guided to meet more joyful people and do more things that give me joy. I thank God for joyful experiences.

AFFIRMATION

I have more joyful experiences in my life now.

MY JOB, EMPLOYMENT, CAREER

I was born with a gift, a talent that can only be expressed by me. Of the billions of people on the Earth, each one has a unique talent. My gift my talent is uniquely mine. There is no competition in the expression of my gift and talent. No one can duplicate my innate gift. My gift, my talent, is my birthright to express. My gift, my talent, is God-given to me only. I may be expressing my gift now, or I may be in a preparation mode of developing my talent or gift for expressing later in my life. Nonetheless, I have a powerful and wonderful gift and talent that blesses me and others.

The best way to find, identify, and grow my talent is to do the very best at what I am doing now. My talent can best be found by identifying what I enjoy doing. What makes me happy and joyful? Is it serving others, or is it creating something?

To further help me to identify my talent and gift, in my quiet moments I sit down and write out what I would like to do. I put as much detail in this as I can. I include the kind of people that I would like to work with or be around, and I include the place or locations in which I would like to do it.

I always include the amount of money that I desire to make. I go over my list daily, or several times a day. I revise or add to this list. I see and feel myself doing this daily.

I am an individualized, unique creation of God. I deserve the best of all things. I deserve happiness, peace of mind, respect, love, financial prosperity, and all good. I remember I am the creator of my life, and no one has been given charge of creating my life except me. God within me guides me. I look within for my answers, not outside of me. This is taking responsibility for myself.

If one job ends, I celebrate the end and know it is just the beginning of something new and wonderful for me. I know that I have completed what I needed to there, and it is time to move forward into the next opportunity. I do not spend one moment in sadness, anger, or regret—*I move forward. I create my new experience.*

AFFIRMATION

I am now happily doing exactly what I enjoy doing in my work and career. I am so blessed to do the type of work that I enjoy. I make a good living doing exactly what I enjoy doing. I am happy and fulfilled in my work.

MY MONEY

————— •❖• —————

I give thanks for the financial affairs that I presently have. I
know that the money that I have is a blessing to me. I set up
my lifestyle according to my own blessed financial income,
not according to what anyone else has.

I speak only good thoughts about my money. I am thankful,
and I know that my thoughts create my circumstances. I always
remember this principle. I understand that the money that
I presently have is a reflection of my thinking, whether my
thinking is of abundance or poverty. If I choose to increase my
income, I look for new opportunities to do so. As I develop
and sharpen my skills, becoming more effective and efficient
at my present work or career, I recognize new money-making
opportunities. I make myself valuable and become the best I
can be in what I am doing. Others recognize that and help me
to move forward. I have value, and I believe in myself.

My Creator has blessed me with wonderful talents and
abilities. I enhance my present talents to attract greater
opportunities that bring me the income that I desire. My
Creator connects me with all the right and perfect people that

allow me to develop and use my God-given talents and abilities. God has unlimited and wonderful ways in which financial blessings flow to me. I am thankful for my present financial affairs and my future financial affairs. Money is a tool for me to use to have the things I desire. I desire things that are beneficial to me and others.

The creative forces of the universe have unlimited ways in which I can be blessed financially. I can be blessed by performing some type of work or by some wonderful financial gift. I stay open and receptive to my financial blessings, which come in expected and unexpected ways. My financial income continues to increase.

I feel good about money and having money. If a negative thought enters my mind, I immediately let it go and replace it with a positive thought. I do not engage in negative thinking with others. I remove myself from conversations about lack and negativity about money.

My financial affairs are sustained by God, the giver of my financial affairs.

I enjoy financial peace of mind.

I have a large, steady, dependable, permanent financial income now.

I let go of limiting ways of thinking that have held me back in the past. I give thanks for my unlimited thoughts about money, which are moving me forward into financial freedom.

I am thankful that I now understand that I can co-create my financial affairs and life with the creative energy of the universe through the power of my thoughts and words.

AFFIRMATION

I live within my income. I am thankful for all the money that I now have. I give thanks for more and more money coming to me in expected and unexpected wonderful ways.

I now have plenty of money to share, spare, and save.

I enjoy divine order in my financial affairs and wisdom in my spending, saving, and investing.

MY FOOD

———— ▪ ✸ ▪ ————

Healthy food is the fuel for my body. I now choose healthy and nutritional food for my body. My body is how I transport myself in my daily activities. Just as a car needs the proper type of fuel to operate, my body needs the proper type of food to remain healthy. I educate myself about good food choices. My good food choices energize me and promote my good health. I now make good food choices. I enjoy the food choices that I make. I feel vibrant and strong as I continue with my healthy food choices.

I enjoy fresh vegetables and fruits often. I enjoy learning new ways of preparing fresh vegetables and fruits. I am amazed by how tasty and filling my new food choices are to me.

I now attract into my life people that share delicious and healthy food and recipes with me. I enjoy these healthy recipes and the new friendships that I make. We exchange recipes and provide encouragement to each other for healthy eating.

Every nerve, muscle, organ, and cell in my body radiates perfect health because of my healthy food choices. I feel vibrant, strong, and healthy each day as I carry out my daily activities.

My new food choices help me to attain and maintain my healthy body weight. I enjoy daily exercises. My daily exercise helps me to move easily and freely as I perform my daily activities.

I enjoy gardening. Whether in a pot on my patio or in my yard, I enjoy growing fresh vegetables and fruits. I enjoy watching my fruits and vegetables grow. This is nature in action. This makes me feel closer to my Creator. I am excited about my good health.

AFFIRMATION

I feel energetic and strong every day as I go about my daily activities.

My new food choices help me have a strong, healthy body.

MY GRIEF

———•—❁—•———

When the death of a loved one occurs, be it expected or sudden, we are often not prepared for the loss. Missing the presence of a loved one can be a sad experience. The loss of a loved one leaves a void in my life. Regardless of the person's age, it seems too soon. The normal emotions are denial and anger, and then we come to the realization that this is our new reality, living without our loved ones. Then it is time to figure out what we can learn from this experience.

Looking deeply into life can bring understanding and comfort. We come into life with the expectation of a long, fulfilling life, but sometimes that promise is not fulfilled.

Let us remember that we are spiritual beings having human experiences. We come to Earth to learn life lessons of love, compassion, helpfulness to others, forgiveness, and more. However, the primary reason we are here is to understand life, how it works, our purpose, and the reason we are here. Let us remember that life on Earth is not a permanent dwelling place. None of us come to stay. Life on Earth is temporary. We come from somewhere else, stay for a while, and then we return to the place from which we came.

The Creator, who we call God, never loses charge of anything for God is in all things, and God is within us. We could never be different from the one who created us. God is Spirit, and our spirits are the part of God that dwells within us. If you can dismiss for a while the idea of heaven and hell and replace it with a forever loving father-mother God, who gives us life, who welcomes us home when we pass from this life, then the idea of passing or discarding the earthly body can be very comforting.

We all will return home one day. We will all return to the loving arms of our Creator, family, and friends who have gone home before us.

When a loved one passes, I now celebrate their life. I celebrate the opportunity to love them . I celebrate all that I have learned from that person. I celebrate all of the accomplishments that person has made. I celebrate that they have gone home.

This concept lessens the feeling of loss and provides a higher understanding of death of the physical body. I will miss my loved one, but I take comfort in the fact that I will see them again, and that person will welcome me home when it is time for me to return.

If my loved one could speak to me, they would tell me to continue my life, and fill the void with loving others. Do not waste time grieving, but spend my time doing what I'm supposed to do in this temporary life. I remember the good times that I had with my loved one; I remember the laughter and fun times. I have my memories, but I do not live in my memories. My loved one will always live within my memories of them . I am thankful that they were a part of my life at that time. I am thankful for the many ways in which that person blessed my life with their love, compassion, understanding, wisdom, laughter, and fun, but I move on. There is so much more for me to do while I am here.

My loved one is okay. My loved one wants me to be okay and go on with my life. So I will be strong. I look for opportunities to love and be helpful to others.

AFFIRMATION

I trust God in his infinite wisdom that my loved one is safe and secure with God in her heavenly home. I believe that I will see my loved one again. I am comforted by this thought, and I move forward with my life, loving others and being helpful to others.

MY LIFE

M y life is renewed by renewing my thinking. With persistence and a strong desire to understand more clearly my relationship to my Creator, I have moved forward into a happier, healthier, and more peaceful lifestyle. Many other people have been channels through which my Creator has encouraged me, inspired me, and provided me with a clear understanding of myself and my relationship to others.

I have forgiven those whom I previously felt harmed by; I have learned to respect others when we share different opinions; I have learned to love others despite our differences; I have learned to treat others in the way that I would like to be treated; I have learned that what I desire is what God desires for me; I have learned that being thankful for the little things and the big things in my life keeps me aware that God is the source of all things; I have learned to always be my best self in all situations; I have learned that I can achieve the goals that I strive for with a steadfast determination; I have learned that with faith, the desires of my heart will unfold; I have learned that God is always with me as a constant companion, guiding and directing my journey; I have learned that loving myself allows me to love others; I have learned that I am a spiritual being first, and I am having a human experience on planet Earth; and I have learned that I can relax and do my part, and God has everything under control even when things appear out of control.

I have learned these things and more. As I continue to move forward in my life, I remain open and receptive to my growth and progress, always aware that the one that created me is always with me to help and guide me, and that I am never alone.

AFFIRMATION

With God's guidance, I can accomplish my life goals.

MY PROTECTION

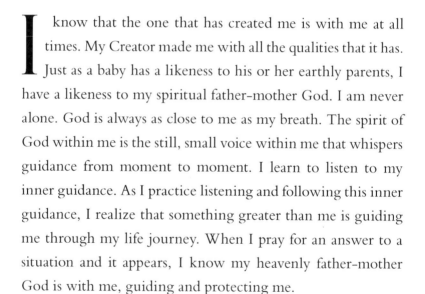

I know that the one that has created me is with me at all times. My Creator made me with all the qualities that it has. Just as a baby has a likeness to his or her earthly parents, I have a likeness to my spiritual father-mother God. I am never alone. God is always as close to me as my breath. The spirit of God within me is the still, small voice within me that whispers guidance from moment to moment. I learn to listen to my inner guidance. As I practice listening and following this inner guidance, I realize that something greater than me is guiding me through my life journey. When I pray for an answer to a situation and it appears, I know my heavenly father-mother God is with me, guiding and protecting me.

Divine protection is always with me whether I am aware of it or not. I am kept safe in all situations. I am protected by divine protection at all times. I am thankful to my indwelling father-mother God for my personal divine protection at all times.

If I feel fearful, I remember there is nothing to fear, that God is always with me, protecting me. I remember that fear is a thought, and thoughts have power. I immediately decide not to give anymore thought to fear. I replace thoughts of fear with thoughts of God's divine protection over me. As I focus on God divine protection over me, thoughts of fear vanish into the sea of nothingness. I now feel safe and secure. As I focus on God's divine protection over me, I am guided to go places and do things that keep me safe and secure.

AFFIRMATION

I am divinely protected at all times in all situations. My loved ones are divinely protected at all times in all situations. I fear not because my father-mother God is always with me and my loved ones, guiding and protecting us at all times in all situations. I am free of fear.

MY GRACE

---·-✺-·---

When I think of grace, I think of a blessing that has come to me unearned. In my open and receptive state of mind, I am blessed by the grace of God. It could be an expected blessing or an unexpected blessing. Realizing the meaning of grace, I now become more open and receptive to receiving an inflow of blessings from the universe. I ask that God's grace be upon me in wonderful ways. If I'd like to have more wonderful, genuine friends to enjoy, I now open up to God's grace to bless me in that way. If I would like to have that dream job, I open up to God's grace to grant me that opportunity. If I would like to have a life partner with whom I can enjoy and have a family with, I open up now to that blessing coming to me. If I would like to have peace of mind in my life, I now open up to the way that can happen to me. If I would like to have my own business doing work that I enjoy, I now open up to that experience in my life. If I would like to have an increase in my financial affairs, I open up to recognizing opportunities that bring more money to me. If I would like for my children to be better behaved or better students in school, I look for resources that can help me to achieve this.

Now that I realize that there is nothing too hard for the universe to deliver and that I do not have to be deserving of it, I now open up to the manifestation of grace in my life, my world, and in all of my affairs. I may be guided to go somewhere that I normally do not go to meet this blessing. I may receive an unexpected call that blesses me. I may read something that catches my attention, and there lies my answer. I may meet a friend or stranger that shares something with me that directs me to what I am looking for. The universe has unlimited ways to connect me with my heart's desire. So I now put my faith in that great, amazing power and let myself be blessed by the grace of God. In doing so I discover my life becomes less stressful and easier every day.

AFFIRMATION

God's grace in my life is sufficient for me.

MY THANKFULNESS

A s I reflect on my life, I am filled with thankfulness. As I think about my past and all the people in my life that have been an inspiration to me, I am thankful. It could have been my parents, a teacher, a friend, a neighbor, a minister, a counselor, or a stranger who unknowingly gave me words of encouragement that lifted my spirit at a time when I needed it most.

I look at where I am today in my life. I walk around my house, and I am thankful for the beautiful environment in which I live; I am thankful for my home, its furnishings, and the clothes that I wear.

I look at my finances, and I am thankful for the work that I do that helps me to live in the way that I do. I am thankful that I am able to keep my bills paid and have extra money to do the things that I enjoy.

I look at my relationships, and I am thankful for my family, friends, coworkers, and associates and our harmonious relationships. I am thankful for their supportiveness of me and my supportiveness of them.

I am thankful for my health. I am thankful that I have been guided to change my diet to a healthy diet that promotes my good health. I am thankful that I have been inspired to exercise daily and enjoy a strong, healthy body.

I am thankful for my spiritual growth, my awareness of God, and my relationship to God. I am thankful for being aware of the partnership that I have with God, which makes my life so much easier and happier with peace of mind.

As I think on all of these things, I am overwhelmed with feelings of thanksgiving. My thankfulness and gratitude opens me up to giving and receiving more good in my life. My just enough turns into abundance, and my abundance turns into a wealth of love, helpfulness, encouragement, support, money, and success in my life, my world, and in all of my affairs.

AFFIRMATION

I am overwhelmed with thankfulness. I thank you, God, for everything.

MY GOALS AND DREAMS

s I review and evaluate where my life is now, ideas come up in my mind that excite me. I think of something that I would enjoy and like to do. At that moment a goal and dream is born. I remember that my first step is to have faith that I can accomplish this. I treat this newborn idea as I would treat a newborn baby. I protect this idea by only sharing it with friends or family that would be supportive of me. This strengthens my faith and belief that I can really do this.

I begin to develop my action plan of fulfilling my goal and dream. It may be going to school, opening a business, traveling, getting married, having children, or retiring. As I develop my plan, I carefully think about all that it would take to manifest this dream. I think of my finances, my health, my family, and anything or anyone that might be affected by me realizing this dream.

As I continue to move forward in the realization of my dream, I thank God for the idea, and I ask for guidance in the development of my dream. I ask that I be guided to everybody and everything that will help my dream unfold. As people and things are presented to me, I recognize that I am being guided and directed to the fulfillment of my dream. If I lose my focus, I go back to God for guidance and direction.

As I meditate upon guidance and direction, I receive inspiration from insights of my own or direction from others of what to do next. I know that timing is important in the unfoldment of my dream. There may be times when I need to accelerate my actions, and there may be times for me to develop a slower pace in the unfoldment of my dream. I realize that God, my Creator, my giver of the dream, my partner in it all, is guiding me to perfect unfoldment at the perfect time.

I remain thankful, happy, and excited as I proceed to the unfoldment of my dream. I keep an unwavering faith through the whole process. I stay open to all opportunities that come to me that are a part of my dream.

When my dream manifests, I am so thankful for its unfoldment and the joy that it brings to me and others. I remember the road map, the steps that I took for my dream to unfold, so when I embark upon another dream or goal, I always take God as my partner. I am thankful for this realization.

AFFIRMATION

Thank you, God, for the perfect and wonderful unfoldment of my dreams and goals and placing all the wonderful people, places, events, and opportunities in my life.

MY FORGIVENESS

I now realize that being unforgiving means withdrawing *love* or holding it back. I also realize that when I am holding back love from someone because of something she said or did, that only affects me. Withholding love creates a negative emotion within me. Negative emotions can be harmful to me. With my new realization, I now release all and any unforgiveness that I may have been holding against anyone or anything. With this release of unforgiveness, I feel a great sense of freedom. I feel as if I have been released from a heavy weight. I thank God for the idea of forgiveness, for what it means and what it has done for me.

I now absolutely forgive everyone in my life and everything that has ever offended me and everyone and everything that I have offended forgives me now. I am now set free to love everyone. Forgiveness frees me.

The freedom that I now feel for forgiving opens up new freedoms for me to explore, new possibilities and opportunities for me to prosper in my life, my world, and in all of my affairs. Now when someone says something that could be offensive to me, I no longer take it personally; I stop and realize that something is not going well in her life, and I find a loving and understanding way to respond to her. This reaction always gets the person's attention, causing her to rethink her actions either now or later. This way of least resistance helps me keep my peace of mind.

As I now move through life with my renewed thinking, instead of holding a grudge, I love and receive love in return. I now move through life with a loving and understanding spirit. I am renewed by the renewal of my thinking.

AFFIRMATION

I now forgive everything and everybody in my life that has offended me and everything and everybody that I have offended forgives me. I now go free with a renewed understanding and loving spirit.

MY UNDERSTANDING

Life can sometimes be complicated, confusing, and frustrating without an understanding of life and how it works. Life can be exciting, happy, and fulfilling when I understand the basic principles of life and use them in my everyday experiences. Understanding flows to me in wonderful ways. My understanding might come from a family member, a friend, a stranger, a television program, the Internet, my own personal insight, or in some other wonderful way.. As I seek understanding, it is provided to me.

As I seek to understand myself, I gain understanding of others. I understand that when I need an answer to a situation, I simply ask for the right answer and am patient until it appears. The universe will always respond to me. Exercising patience in situations helps me to remain calm and peaceful instead of anxious and stressed.

Understanding gives me peace of mind. When I am faced with a situation where a person is being disrespectful toward me, I first stop and think. Usually, the person is venting frustration or anger, but not because of anything that I have done. I have learned not to take this type of situation personally. I listen and watch, and when the person has let it out, I know that he or she is dealing with another issue and not with me. I respond to that person in a kind and loving way, which diffuses her anger or frustration. It is like pouring water on a fire. I immediately see a transformation in that person's attitude, which is followed by an apology either then or later. It is my understanding of people that allows my life to be peaceful and happy. I bless others and myself because of my understanding.

I realize that life is about lessons. Situations are teachers to me. Looking at life as a school gives me a better understanding of situations. I look for the life lessons in every situation instead of resisting them. This helps promote my growth. I know that resisting lessons by refusing to accept them as learning experiences just delays my growth. I now welcome opportunities to grow and become all that I can be.

AFFIRMATION

I am open and receptive to learning my lessons so I can move forward with my life. My understanding of life sets me free to grow.

MY DIVINE PLAN

I believe that my life has a purpose. I believe that there is a divine plan for my life that includes happiness, love, joy, peace of mind, and fulfillment. If I do not yet realize the fullness of the divine plan for my life, I know that I am a work in progress. I realize that what I am presently doing is preparing me to do greater things. Right now, right where I am, I do my very best so that I can advance forward in my life.

No matter how things seem to be, I keep my faith in the unfoldment of the divine plan for my life. I put thought into situations and make wise decisions and choices. I use my intuition. When I feel something or someone is right for me, I follow that feeling. I know that this feeling is God within me guiding me in the right direction. This divine guidance always points me in the right direction to do the best thing for myself. If I see that I did not make the best decision or choice, I know that it was a learning situation and that I can correct it and start anew. I remember life is like a school. I learn my lessons so that I can move forward.

As I learn to follow my divine guidance, I recognize the unfoldment of the divine plan for my life. Being happy is a part of the divine plan for my life. I now make choices that include my happiness. I now make choices that include my peace of mind. I now make choices that include true love for me. I now make choices that include my financial well-being. I now make choices that include my good health. I now make choices that include loving relationships. I now am enjoying a fulfilling life doing the things that I enjoy. I now am enjoying the fulfillment of the divine plan of my life. I am thankful to God for guiding me to such a wonderful place in my life.

AFFIRMATION

I thank God for the unfoldment of the divine plan for my life, which fills my life with happiness, love, peace of mind, joy, and complete fulfillment.

MY ANSWERED PRAYERS

I rejoice, rejoice, and rejoice in my answered prayers. There is no greater jubilation in life than my answered prayers. I am filled with excitement, joy, and a great deal of thankfulness to the universe for bringing forth the answer to my prayers. God has given me the desire of my heart. I know that which I have desired God has desired for me too. I remained open and receptive to my heart's desire, and God found the perfect way to bring it to me. The happiness that I now am experiencing is far beyond what I could imagine. My answered prayer exceeds my greatest expectation. My answered prayer makes my life so fulfilling in every way. The outcome of my answered prayer is perfect for me.

While praying for a desire, be it a new job, a new business, a soul mate, life partner, a healing, a new home, a new automobile, peace of mind, or wise decision-making or child-rearing skills, I had moments of doubt. When having those moments of doubt, I realized that I must keep the faith. I remembered that God loves me and will open great opportunities to me. I remembered that God can do what I can't do for myself. I remembered that the spirit of God is within me, and that is my partnership with my Creator. I remembered that all things are possible with God. I remembered that God has answered prayers for me in my past, and he will see me through all situations. I remember that all things are possible with God. I remember that God does not give to me because I deserve it, but because God loves me. I remember that if I do not have my prayer answered now, the universe is gathering all the right and perfect people, circumstances, and conditions to answer my prayer. I remember that God gives me signs that my answered prayer is coming when I hear of or see someone else receiving their answered prayer; I then know my answered prayer is near.

I remembered just before my prayer was answered that I let go and let God handle the manifestation. At that time I remembered that I can do nothing, and God can do all. When I let go and let God, I felt a deep peace and calm about my prayer being answered. When I let go and let God, I felt that something greater than me working for my highest good.

AFFIRMATION

Thank you, God, for my answered prayers. Thank you for my new understanding of our relationship and my partnership with you as my prayer answerer.

CONCLUSION

T he prayers in this book have come to me as inspirations to share with you. As they come through me as I too am inspired and blessed. It is my deepest desire to share with you these ideas and beliefs that have worked beautifully in my life.

Life comes with challenges, but it also comes with answers to those challenges. When you become aware of how to seek those answers, life smoothes out and becomes a very happy and rewarding experience.

As you establish that partnership with your Creator, your God, something greater than you, you begin to find something that you can depend on. This is a life-changing discovery. This is the spiritual part of you. Your relationship with God is built experience by experience. Each experience will deepen and strengthen your relationship. Each experience provides you with a very intimate relationship with your Creator. You will gradually know that there is something that is working on your behalf in life. You will begin to trust its existence. As you ask

God and receive your blessings, you will begin to understand how life works.

Remember that people, places, conditions, situations, and circumstance are *channels* through which God talks to you, comforts you, and answers your prayers. This universal power and presence within you is what guides you daily whether you are aware of it or not. God is always with you. When you pray and when you do not pray, God is with you.

The laws of life work for you whether you are aware of them or understand them or not. You may not know how electricity works, but it works without your understanding of it. When you flip the switch, the lights come on. When you flip the switch of your thinking to positive, God-filled thoughts, your life comes on.

Keep your thoughts and words positive and uplifting for yourself and for others.

God is as close to you as your breath. Acknowledge the presence of God in all that you do, and He will guide your way.

You have the power of God within you; consciously use it and have a great, happy, wonderful life.

Empower yourself,
Gwendolyn L. Roberts

ABOUT THE AUTHOR

————◆❋◆————

Gwendolyn (Gwen) L. Roberts is a native to Charlotte, North Carolina. She is the firstborn of loving parents JC and Lillian Roberts. She and her siblings, James, Sandra, and Malcolm, enjoyed a normal happy childhood and were raised in the traditional Baptist church.

Prior to college graduation, Gwen experienced a life-changing experience of the death of her fiancée. This began Gwen's active pursuit to understand life. What is this thing called life? Why are we here? What is my purpose? What is death? What is the purpose of it all?

After college graduation, Gwen relocated to Atlanta, Georgia, which was the beginning of her active spiritual journey. Gwen's life questions began to unravel as she read and studied extensively many spiritually-focused books. After several years she taught various classes on truth principles and spirituality.

As a sociology and psychology major in college, Gwen's life work has been helping others by working for a variety human service agencies over thirty years. This she felt was her life calling, not realizing that these experiences, challenges, and opportunities were setting the framework for the work she is doing today as a real estate broker, spiritual teacher, and spiritual writer. Her social work brought into focus for her the importance of one's spirituality. She constantly saw how one's thinking was always parallel to one's circumstances as well as her own.

In 1981, Gwen relocated to her hometown Charlotte, North Carolina. Actively using truth principles and affirmations, she attracted her dream job and simultaneously founded and opened the Truth Institute in Charlotte, where she continued to teach classes on truth principles and spirituality.

After two marriages, at age forty-three Gwen realized that having her own family was important and the next focus for her. As a single parent, she was inspired to adopt a healthy, happy baby boy. When Brandon realized that he did not have a father like his other seven-year-old classmates, Gwen and Brandon went to the only sources they knew—God and affirmative prayer—to bring the right and perfect father and husband to them. Today, Gwen, Bruce, Brandon, April B., April F., Rian, Sean, Keisha, and Stephanie enjoy a happy, God-given blended family. Although all of the children are adults with their own families now, we continue to connect with each other on various occasions and love each other dearly.

According to Gwen, life has been and continues to be a wonderful spiritual journey. At age sixty-nine, Gwen now is embarking on another career journey as a published author. According to Gwen, her writings are divinely inspired, based upon her studies and personal experiences with life. After nearly fifty years of studying spirituality and affirming her way through life with divine guidance, Gwen decided to share her version of life with you in *Pocket Prayers*. The intent is to inspire you to make your life as fulfilling as you chose for it to be.

Printed in the United States
By Bookmasters